# CLOSE TO
# EXTINCTION

© Aladdin Books Ltd 1991

*First published in the
United States in 1992 by*
Gloucester Press
95 Madison Avenue
New York, NY 10016

ISBN 0-531-17383-6

Library of Congress Catalog
Card Number 88-50522

Printed in Belgium

The original edition of this book was published in the **Survival** series.

The front cover photograph shows a puma, or mountain lion, surveying its territory. Pumas are endangered in some parts of North America.

# Contents

# CLOSE TO EXTINCTION

## John A Burton

Gloucester Press

New York : London : Toronto : Sydney

# Introduction

Extinction is a natural process. As species become extinct they are replaced by other species, which are more suited to a particular environment. All species become extinct sooner or later. Even humans could become extinct.

At one time people thought that the world was created recently and that the creatures living on Earth were all created at the same time. Although many still believe in creation myths, modern scientists think that the planet Earth is millions of years old. They believe it has been inhabited by living plants and animals for at least 5 billion years. Plants and animals are thought to be evolving – that is to say gradually changing – into new species. As this process goes on, some species become extinct.

Millions of years ago, Earth was inhabited by very different species. The most famous of these were the dinosaurs. They roamed the earth for tens of millions of years, but eventually died out and were replaced by different species, including birds and mammals. In the past there was time for species to evolve as others became extinct. However, during the past 5,000 years humans have become more and more destructive. Humans have hunted some species to extinction and are now destroying the habitats of many thousands of others.

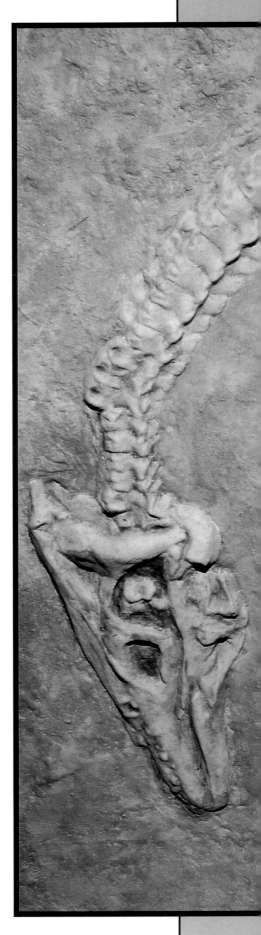

▷ *Plesiosaurus macrocephalus* is an extinct marine reptile which inhabited the seas that once covered where Britain is now. It lived some 180 million years ago, from the late Triassic Period to the early Jurassic Period. Plesiosaurs were long-necked and carnivorous (meat-eating), growing up to 40 feet long. Their fossils are often remarkably well preserved, because when they died their bodies were covered in fine mud which preserved them.

We share the planet Earth with between five and ten million species of living things. Animals and plants have become extinct in nearly all parts of the world, and there are species on the brink of extinction practically everywhere. However, it is on islands that the greatest number of species have been wiped out recently. Many islands have very distinctive plants and animals. For instance, hutias are large rodents confined to the West Indies, where several species are endangered, or perhaps extinct. Many islands in the Pacific have endangered species living on them. On Samoa, the wood rail was last seen in the 1870s, and the flying fox has declined rapidly and may become extinct. On the islands of Hawaii there were once 22 species of the honeycreeper bird – nine are now extinct together with many other species of birds. In the Indian Ocean, the islands of Mauritius, Reunion and Rodriguez had large flightless birds. These are now extinct.

Korea
X Crested Shellduck

Bering Strait
X Steller's S

China
E Golden Slipper Orchid

Japan
X Japanese Wolf
E Japanese Sea Lion
E Oriental White Stork
E Short-tailed Albatross

Asia
E Asian Elephant
E Asiatic Lion
E Javan Rhinoceros
E Sumatran Rhinoceros
E Tiger
E Snow Leopard

Hawaiian Islar
X 28 species

Borneo
E Rafflesia

Samoa
X Samoan Wood R
E Samoan Flying Fo

Australia
X Dwarf Emu
E Bridled Nailtail Wallaby

Philip Island
E Philip Island

Tasmania
X Thylacine

New Zealand
X Moas
E South Island Kokako

△ The map shows just a few of the animals and plants that have become extinct since the year 1600, or may become extinct in the near future.

◁ The thylacine, or marsupial wolf, once occurred widely on Tasmania, and also the mainland of Australia. Although occasionally reported, it probably became extinct about 50 years ago.

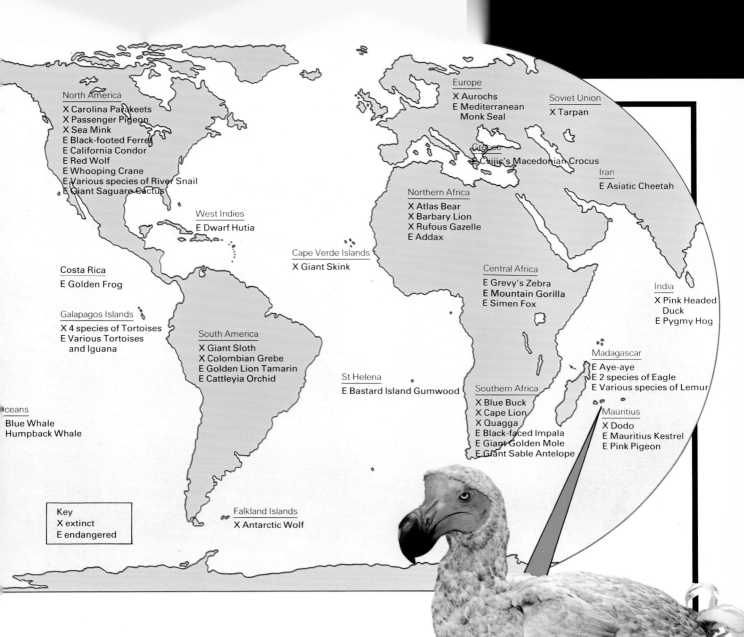

North America
X Carolina Parakeets
X Passenger Pigeon
X Sea Mink
E Black-footed Ferret
E California Condor
E Red Wolf
E Whooping Crane
E Various species of River Snail
E Giant Saguaro Cactus

West Indies
E Dwarf Hutia

Costa Rica
E Golden Frog

Galapagos Islands
X 4 species of Tortoises
E Various Tortoises
and Iguana

South America
X Giant Sloth
X Colombian Grebe
E Golden Lion Tamarin
E Cattleyia Orchid

Oceans
Blue Whale
Humback Whale

Cape Verde Islands
X Giant Skink

St Helena
E Bastard Island Gumwood

Falkland Islands
X Antarctic Wolf

Europe
X Aurochs
E Mediterranean
Monk Seal

Greece
E Cvijic's Macedonian Crocus

Northern Africa
X Atlas Bear
X Barbary Lion
X Rufous Gazelle
E Addax

Central Africa
E Grevy's Zebra
E Mountain Gorilla
E Simen Fox

Southern Africa
X Blue Buck
X Cape Lion
X Quagga
E Black-faced Impala
E Giant Golden Mole
E Giant Sable Antelope

Soviet Union
X Tarpan

Iran
E Asiatic Cheetah

India
X Pink Headed
Duck
E Pygmy Hog

Madagascar
E Aye-aye
E 2 species of Eagle
E Various species of Lemur

Mauritius
X Dodo
E Mauritius Kestrel
E Pink Pigeon

Key
X extinct
E endangered

Because of the dense and often rapidly growing human populations, many species of large mammals are threatened. These include elephants, lions, rhinoceroses and tigers. The quagga (a type of zebra), blue buck, tarpan, rufous gazelle, and giant sloth are just a few of the animals that have been exterminated by humans. In the future it is thought that in order to protect species, we will need to have programs which protect the environment as a whole rather than ones aimed at individual species. We need to ensure the survival of the great variety of animal and plant species on Earth.

△ The dodo became extinct about 1680. It was a large, flightless bird.

7

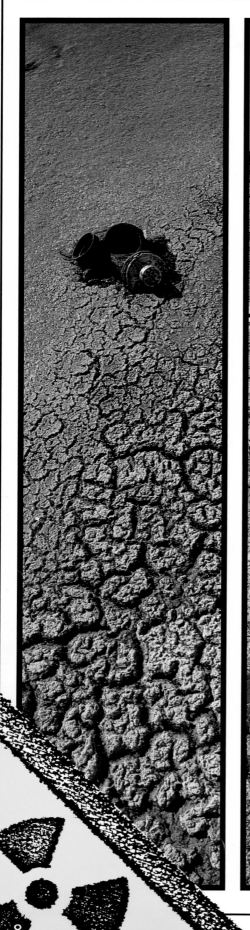

# Human devastation

◁ In the past 40 years, many nuclear bombs have been exploded on islands in the Pacific Ocean, despite opposition from the people who live there. The French continued to test nuclear devices until the 1980s. The effects of nuclear radiation will continue to poison the wildlife and people in the area, and will certainly cause long-term genetic defects.

"We have reached a desperate situation in the second half of the 20th century, when one species – Homo Sapiens – is responsible for the current catastrophic increase in the rate of species extinction."

Sir Peter Scott, Naturalist

The activities of people have always affected wildlife. At first humans survived by hunting animals and gathering roots, seeds and other parts of plants. But there were so few humans that they had very little effect on the other wildlife. When humans started to farm the land and tame animals for their own use, they had to start killing any animals that might take their crops or kill their livestock. They started to attack whole species: in Europe, lions, wolves and bears were hunted until they only survived in remote places. But by 1600 very few entire species had been wiped out by humans.

From 1600, as Europeans improved their guns and colonized other parts of the world, the rate of extinctions increased. Then, as the human population grew, so did the demand for farmland, wood, metals and other raw materials. Many of the world's natural places were destroyed, together with the wildlife that lived in them. The greatest numbers of wild animals and plants now live in the tropical forests of Asia, Africa and South America, and it is here that they face the greatest threat.

◁ As forests, such as this one in tropical Malaya, are cut down, thousands of other plants and animals are killed at the same time. The areas that have been cleared of forest in many parts of the tropics are so extensive that many species are threatened and scientists also think it may be affecting the world's climate.

# North America

Although the European settlers have destroyed much of the wildlife of North America, the American Indians, who settled North America 30,000 years before the Europeans, were probably also responsible for the extinction of some species. They hunted giant sloths and probably mastodons (extinct elephants). However, since the Europeans arrived in the New World, the rate of extinction has certainly accelerated. The passenger pigeon is believed to have been the most numerous bird in the world. They were hunted ceaselessly and in 1914 the last one died in an American zoo.

▽ Bison (buffalo) once numbered millions, and roamed from the Canadian Arctic south through the plains to Mexico. As the railroads spread west, the bison were slaughtered and often left to rot. By the late 1800s they were nearly extinct, but a few were preserved and now their numbers are building up. Conservationists have made proposals to establish a huge reserve for them in the plains of the United States.

" The story of what the white man has done to the continent's wealth of wildlife is not a pleasant one."

Richard H Pough

The California condor is North America's rarest bird. Hunted because it was thought to be a menace to livestock, the last remaining birds are being kept in zoos and bred in a special recovery program. Two were released into the wild in 1992. The endangered whooping crane is building up its numbers, and by the early 1990s there were close to 150 in the wild, and more in captivity.

The Mexican grizzly bear used to occupy an enormous range from Arizona to California. Despite protection laws it was hunted in the 1950s and was thought to be extinct. In 1969 a few survivors were found in northwest Mexico.

△ The bald eagle is the national emblem of the United States, but was exterminated over a large part of its range by shooting and poisoning.

▽ The black-footed ferret is one of North America's rarest mammals. Although it is extinct in the wild, by 1991 there were 200 in captivity, with plans to reintroduce these to the prairies.

11

# South America

Until the 20th century most of tropical America was only inhabited by scattered tribes of Amerindians. European settlements were largely confined to the coasts.

Almost half of the world's rain forests lie in Brazil. Most of the Amazon and its wildlife was remote and inaccessible, with huge tracts undisturbed and unexplored. However, in the last quarter of a century, roads have begun to crisscross this wilderness giving access to people and their machines. The greatest damage to wildlife comes from the lumber companies, ranchers and landless farmers, who clear the forests. Once the trees have been cut down, they are rarely replaced. The land is sometimes used for agriculture but often loses what little fertility it had in a short time.

The remaining pieces of virgin forest become isolated. Orchids and other rare plants become confined to small areas where they can easily be wiped out by people searching for extremely expensive rarities for plant collectors.

▽ Jaguar became fashionable for fur coats and other items in the 1960s (see below). As they became rarer, furriers turned to other species, such as the ocelot. An ocelot (illustrated here) is only half the size of a jaguar. As ocelots became rarer, smaller species such as the margay and Geoffroy's cat were exploited. Although they all still occur over a large range in Central and South America, most of them are now extinct or rare in all the areas close to human settlements.

△ The golden frog had a very restricted range in the cloud forests of Costa Rica. In 1990, scientists announced that the species was possibly extinct. Although the reasons for this are not known for certain, it has been suggested that the cause may be global warming. Worldwide, many species of frogs and other amphibians appear to be declining.

Illegal traders search for rare monkeys, parrots, fish, and other wildlife to sell to zoos and private collectors. Other threats to wildlife come from commercial trappers hunting caimans and snakes (such as the giant-sized anaconda) for their skins. Fortunately all the countries in South America belong to the Convention on International Trade in Endangered Species of Wild Fauna and Flora (CITES). This is helping to prevent the illegal export of wildlife. However, there is a thriving illegal trade in caiman skins. In some countries, for example, forged export documents have been used to ship protected species or their skins overseas.

**The Amazonian forest**
Amazonia contains over three million sq miles of tropical forest. The timber is worth one trillion US dollars. It contains at least 50,000 species of plants and 20 percent of all known birds. Over the past two decades, more than 25 million acres of tropical forest have been destroyed in Brazilian Amazonia to create cattle pastures.

 # Europe

Humans have been taming Europe's wilderness for over 5,000 years. Many species have been exterminated, or now only survive in remote areas such as mountains. Beavers and bears were last seen in the British Isles in the 12th century, wolves in the 18th century. At the beginning of this century the European bison was close to extinction. They would have died out had not a few collectors, such as the Duke of Bedford, kept a herd of captive bison. Captive animals were gathered together and reintroduced into one of Europe's last primeval forests on the border between Poland and the Soviet Union. Small numbers have now been sent to other reserves. Similarly lynx and beavers are being reintroduced into their former range.

▽ Despite the story of Little Red Riding Hood and similar tales, wolves rarely attack humans. However, they can cause serious damage to livestock, particularly sheep, and because of this wolves have been eliminated over nearly all their range in Europe. They survive in a few areas, notably Eastern Europe, Spain and Italy. Before large predatory species such as wolves can return, it is essential that they have sufficient prey — otherwise they will wander outside their reserves and kill farm animals.

"There is still a chance of saving these vanishing species, but it should be seized at once, since any delay will lengthen the list of those already extinct."

HRH The Prince of the Netherlands

## The lady's slipper orchid

By the 1980s, in Britain, the lady's slipper orchid was confined to a single nature reserve in Yorkshire. In Britain and elsewhere in Europe it was once widespread. It is now rare over much of its previous range.

▽ The bearded vulture is more usually known by its German name of *Lammergeier*, which means bone crusher. It drops bones onto rocks to break them so that it can feed on the marrow. It was hunted to the brink of extinction over most of Europe.

Most of Europe's rare animals and plants are now confined to national parks and nature reserves. Wildlife has become a major industry, and millions of people spend their weekends and vacations looking at wildlife. Today, the most serious threat is the draining of the wetlands and other habitat changes. People's interest in seeing wildlife has led to a demand for conservation. There is pressure on governments to preserve areas rich in wildlife, such as the Camargue in France, the Coto Donano in Spain and the Cairngorms in Scotland. Some of Europe's rarest animals live in the Mediterranean – but sea turtles and monk seals need undisturbed beaches in order to breed. It is difficult to get the right balance between human and animal needs.

▽ The medicinal leech was used in most of Europe until comparatively recently to remove poisoned blood from abscesses. It is still important in medical research because it produces hirudin, which prevents blood clotting. It is now nearly extinct in Europe.

 # Africa

Some 2,000 years ago, many of the animals we now associate with East Africa were abundant in North Africa. Elephants, rhinos, hartebeest, crocodiles, wild donkeys, lions, and ostriches were all much more widespread. But the overgrazing of pastures and the loss of fertility in the soil led to erosion. During the past 2,000 years the Sahara Desert has been steadily growing. The loss of habitat and hunting has eliminated many species from the northern parts of their range, and they are now declining in almost all parts of Africa.

The great herds of plains animals – wildebeest, zebra, eland, gazelles and other antelope, together with the hunting dogs, vultures and jackals which accompanied them – once migrated over vast areas of Africa. The springbok in South Africa numbered millions, but were slaughtered and now find their traditional migration routes blocked by ten feet high wire game fences. Once populations of large conspicuous animals are isolated in small groups, it becomes increasingly easy for poachers to hunt them to extinction.

**Africa's forests**
Tropical Africa has about 675,000 sq miles of tropical forest, of which 580,000 are in Zaire. The forests of East Africa are particularly rich in species: Uganda's forests have 800 species of trees and shrubs (130 exist in all of Europe). In 1900 Kenya had four times as much forest as now.

▽ As recently as the mid-1960s the black rhinoceros was still found in bushy country and open grasslands over most of Africa south of the Sahara. But by the mid-1970s it was beginning to decline rapidly, mostly from poaching for its horn. By the late 1980s, the world population was estimated at under 4,000.

△ The African wild ass, the ancestor of the donkey, is critically endangered. Although once widespread in the grasslands of North Africa, it is now reduced to isolated populations, mostly in extreme desert. Fortunately, there are small numbers in captivity, which may someday be released into a suitable protected area.

Many of Africa's animals continue to decline, and some such as the addax and scimitar-horned oryx are almost extinct. However, nature reserves and national parks are being set aside to protect wildlife. In South Africa the bontebok and mountain zebra have been saved. More parks and reserves are the only solution.

"Africa has the highest (human) population growth rate of any continent. In the never-ending quest for more land to provide a livelihood for more people, wildlife is the loser."

Christoph Imboden, Director, International Council for Bird Preservation

# Madagascar

The wildlife of islands, such as Madagascar, often differs markedly from mainland forms. Many animals are only found on Madagascar. The lemurs are a group of primates once found in Europe, Africa and North America, but long extinct there. On Madagascar about 30 species survived until recently, but several are almost extinct because their forest habitats have been destroyed. Among the many unique groups of animals are the tenrecs (which are similar to shrews and hedgehogs) and chameleons. Many threatened birds are also unique to Madagascar.

- indri habitat
- black lemur habitat
- Verreaux' sifaka habitat

△ The largest of the lemurs, the indris, are confined to the east of Madagascar. They live in trees and are powerful leapers. They are dependent on forests, but these have been extensively reduced by logging. They are now a protected species and live in national parks and reserves.

**The indri**
It grows to a body length of up to 35in and a weight of 15-22 lbs. It has a small tail. Its fur is white and black. It lives in moist forests on hills up to a height of 5,700 feet. It feeds mainly on leaves, fruit and small animals.

### The black lemur
Its body can grow up to 16in in length and its tail up to 20in. It can weigh up to 5 lbs. It lives in humid forests and feeds on leaves, flowers and fruit. It is often bred in captivity in order to prevent its extinction.

△ Black lemurs were once widespread in the humid forests in the north of Madagascar, and on the islands of Nosy Be and Nosy Komba. Nowadays they are mainly found on reserves. Much of their forest habitat has already been destroyed. The species is still threatened by logging, forest fires and the spread of agriculture. Despite protection laws and attempts to control the timber companies, one of its subspecies is already extinct.

◁ Verreaux' sifaka is another member of the indri family. It has a small gliding membrane on its arms to help it leap. Its fur is mainly white with reddish and black patches.

### Verreaux' sifaka
Its body can grow up to 18in in length and its tail to 20in. An adult weighs about 9 lbs. It eats leaves, flowers and unripe fruit, which it peels with its teeth. It lives mainly in forests in reserves and national parks.

Asia has some of the greatest concentrations of people in the world. It has been cultivated by farmers for several thousands of years. The inevitable result has been that much of Asia's wildlife has become rare or extinct. The Asian elephant, three species of rhino, snow leopard, Japanese ibis, two-humped camel, Asiatic wild ass, gharial (a fish-eating crocodile), giant panda, gibbon, lion-tailed macaque, pygmy hog, and several species of wild cattle are among the species which are seriously endangered.

Fortunately in the last few decades considerable efforts have been made to preserve the remaining wildlife. The Chinese have launched a major program to protect pandas. Project Tiger was so successful in India that tigers started to spread outside reserves and prey on cattle, and even attack humans. Gharial eggs have been successfully hatched and released into the wild.

◁ Anti-poaching patrols in Chitawan National Park have been successful in combating the slaughter of elephants, rhinos, tigers and deer.

△ The tiger once ranged over territory from Korea and eastern Siberia to Turkey and south through India and Malaya to much of Indonesia.

## Asia's plants
One of the world's largest plants is also among its rarest. This is the giant Rafflesia which is found in Malaya. Other rare plants of the region include the Chinese slipper orchid and several of the insect-trapping pitcher plants.

WWF

The Philippines contain the greatest concentration of rare species found anywhere in the world, with many species only surviving on a single island, mountain or small area of forest. These range from tiny bats and rodents to the Philippine eagle, and the tamaraw (a wild water buffalo). However, the Philippine forests are being destroyed at an alarming rate.

△ The giant panda was once much more widespread, but its numbers are declining because of its highly specialized diet – it feeds almost exclusively on bamboo, which is dying out in some of the panda reserves. The panda is the symbol of the World Wide Fund for Nature.

 # Australasia

Australia is the largest island in the world and was cut off from Asia millions of years ago, before modern mammals had evolved. The only mammals that reached Australia were marsupials (pouched mammals) and monotremes (egg-layers). These ranged in size from tiny marsupial moles and mice to kangaroos 8 feet high. When Europeans colonized Australia they brought with them domestic and wild animals, which later became pests and competed with the native species.

### Australian plants
Australia was colonized by Europeans in 1788. Since that time, 97 plant species are known to have become extinct. Australia's interior is mainly desert, and because of human activities, the desert is spreading. By 1988, 3,329 species of plant were listed as threatened, of which 209 were classified as endangered.

◁ The scarlet-chested parrot is found in the arid scrublands and open saltbush of Australia. It is nomadic and is usually seen in small groups of up to 10, but occasionally occurs in flocks of 100 or more. It has been extensively trapped for the pet trade. However its numbers fluctuate and after years of rarity it becomes more abundant.

### The scarlet-chested parrot
It grows up to 8 inches in length. It eats seeds exclusively. It lays three to five eggs, usually in a hole in a tree or fallen log. Although it is not immediately threatened, further research is needed.

▷ In January 1983 British botanist, conservationist and TV broadcaster David Bellamy was arrested during a protest against the construction of a dam in Tasmania. The proposed reservoir would have flooded part of one of the last temperate rain forests in the world.

Many of the plants and animals of Australia are adapted to arid conditions and after years of scarcity may suddenly become abundant. If, however, during years of rarity animals are hunted or plants dug up, this may prevent them from increasing their numbers when conditions are right.

One of the most unusual endangered plants in the world is the underground orchid. It is confined to southwest Australia, and apart from occasionally just breaking through the surface of the soil, the entire flower develops underground. The seeds are scattered by native mammals which are attracted by the flower's scent, and disperse them in their droppings.

"Promotion of conservation while neglecting people in poverty can only lead to widespread political unrest."
J. Leigh, R. Boden, J. Briggs,
Extinct and Endangered Plants of Australia, 1984

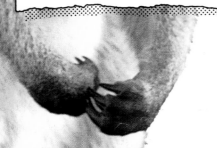

◁ The bridled nail-tail wallaby or flashjack was very common in the 19th century, but by the 1930s was believed to be extinct. However, in 1973 a small colony was discovered in Queensland. It is now fully protected.

# The oceans

Humans have been hunting marine animals, including fish, seals, turtles, and whales, since prehistoric times. Many seals have been hunted so intensely that their numbers have declined and they have been driven away. Now they will only breed on remote islands or inaccessible coasts. Protection has helped some species of seal, such as the northern elephant seal, to increase its numbers to such an extent that they are now a popular tourist attraction in California.

Humans have also hunted whales and dolphins. But it is only in the last 200 years, with steam-powered boats and explosive harpoons, that they have been able to kill many of the larger, faster species. By the 1960s nearly all species of whales had been overhunted, and several were on the brink of extinction. Some, such as the bowhead, have such small populations that scientists believe it may be several centuries before they are safe again.

Perhaps the most remarkable marine mammal is the sea otter, which once occurred from Alaska and the Bering Strait, south to California. It was nearly wiped out because of hunting for its valuable pelt, but is now spreading its range. The manatee and the dugong are both extremely near-sighted and vulnerable to hunters. They are protected, but are still endangered.

"The seas and oceans, and the life that lives in them, are a global common and a global responsibility. Their survival is ultimately critical for the well-being of humanity."

Robert Allen,
International Union for the Conservation of Nature

◁ The dugong, or sea cow, was one of the many victims of the Gulf War of 1991. A massive amount of oil was deliberately allowed to flow into the sea, leaving tens of thousands of birds and other wildlife dead.

◁ Humpback whales make "songs" in order to communicate over great distances in the oceans. Each group of male whales has its own distinctive song. They feed in the cold waters of the Arctic and Antarctic, which are rich in food. In the winter they migrate to warmer waters to breed. After many years of protection their numbers are slowly rebuilding.

◁ Krill is a small crustacean which occurs in huge numbers in the Antarctic Ocean. It provides food for many animals including the Blue Whale. It is now overfished, which threatens those fish which feed on it.

"Ultimately, we are the endangered species. <u>Homo Sapiens</u> is perceived to stand at the top of the pyramid of life, but the pinnacle is a precarious station. We need a large measure of self-consciousness to constantly remind us of the commanding role which we enjoy only at the favor of the web of life that sustains us, that forms a foundation of our total environment....."

Senator Patrick Leahy

△ Poachers are caught by rangers with an impala they have killed. In many parts of Africa poachers are armed with modern automatic weapons, making wildlife protection a dangerous occupation. In many African countries, wildlife has long been an important part of the diet. Wild game animals are easier to raise than domestic species. Wildlife "ranching" could provide people with a cheap source of meat.

# Protection

Wildlife protection involves two main activities: policing and education. Nature reserves need wardens and rangers to look after them, but unless people respect protection laws there is no long-term security for wildlife.

This is why education is important, so that people can understand the reasons for conserving wildlife. It is also essential that people have enough to eat, otherwise it is almost impossible to prevent poaching. In order to stop the cutting down of trees, other fuels for cooking must be available. While millions are starving and billions of dollars are spent on armaments, it is difficult to see how wildlife will survive. The endangered wild ass lives in Ethiopia where a war has torn apart the country, and there are severe food shortages in certain areas.

International treaties are also important in wildlife conservation. By cooperating with each other, countries can protect wildlife. The Convention on the International Trade in Endangered Species of Wild Fauna and Flora (CITES) insists that importing countries have to help stop the trade in protected wildlife. The Convention on Migratory Species (CMS) protects species of birds and other animals when they cross international boundaries. The World Heritage Convention gives protection to places such as the Tasmanian rain forest. When governments sign international treaties, they also have to make sure their laws are adequate.

◁ A baby gorilla was rescued from poachers, who had probably killed its mother in order to obtain the infant. It unfortunately died before it could be released back into the wild. Until recently there was a steady demand from zoos all over the world for young gorillas.

27

# Back from the brink

Although many species continue to decline and are on the brink of extinction, a few have been saved. Pere David's deer, from China, was kept in the Imperial Hunting Park in Peking for about 2,000 years after it became extinct in the wild. It was nearly wiped out during fighting in 1900, but a French missionary, Pere David, had sent some to Europe and the Duke of Bedford managed to breed a herd and save them. In the 1970s they were returned to zoos in China but it was not until 1987 that 40 Pere David's deer were finally released into the wild.

Another captive breeding success story is that of the Hawaiian goose. Because of attacks by domestic animals introduced in Hawaii during the 18th century, there were only 30 left in the wild in the 1950s. By the 1990s there were around 1,500 in captivity and nearly 1,000 in the wild.

"The fact is that no species has ever had such wholesale control over everything on earth, living or dead, as we now have. That lays upon us, whether we like it or not, an awesome responsibility. In our hands now lies not only our own future, but that of all other living creatures with whom we share the earth."

The last lines of "Life on Earth" by David Attenborough

▷ The osprey was extinct in the British Isles, but under strict protection it returned to Scotland and each year it is slowly spreading its range. This is due to the efforts of the Royal Society for the Protection of Birds.

▷ The Arabian oryx was once widespread in the arid regions of the Middle East. It was traditionally hunted by desert nomads on horseback. Modern automatic weapons used from cars led to its near extinction by the 1960s. The Fauna Preservation Society sent an expedition to capture some of the last known animals in the wild. Together with some already in zoos, they were bred until there were sufficient numbers to be released back into the wild. There are now small herds in Oman, and a few other areas in the Middle East.

Until the 1970s the giant redwoods were still being extensively logged for their timber in California. Now there is a huge network of national parks and forest reserves to protect these magnificent trees.

The conservation of the mountain gorilla in the tiny African country of Rwanda has been a great success. In 1979 there were probably only 350 gorillas left in the forests of Central Africa. By promoting tourism so that visitors could see the gorillas, much needed foreign money was brought in. This enabled the national park authorities to enforce protection measures and prevent the poaching that until recently endangered the gorillas. An education program showed the local people the value of both the forests that were protected and the gorillas that live in them.

▷ The bastard island gumwood is a sort of tree daisy, which is confined to the South Atlantic island of St Helena. It was useful for stabilizing sand dunes and preventing erosion. It was nearly brought to extinction by overgrazing. It was reduced to possibly only one specimen, but now over 1,000 seedlings have been cultivated for planting on the island again. The seedlings will help halt erosion and allow other rare plants to recolonize. Once there were over 100 species of plants found only on St Helena. Now only 40 remain.

# Hard facts

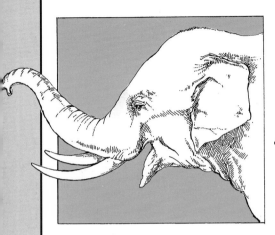

### The Asian elephant
once ranged across southern Asia from the Middle East to Vietnam and south to Malaya. It was hunted for its ivory tusks and it is restricted to small areas. Its numbers are decreasing.

### The pygmy hog
is the world's smallest pig measuring up to 12in at the shoulder. It used to occur in grassy swamps in the foothills of the Himalayas. There are probably less than 150 left now, mainly in Assam.

### The Pyrenean desman
is an aquatic relative of the mole, once widespread in the Pyrenees in France and Spain and other mountains in Spain. Its numbers are now declining because of pollution in its rivers and streams.

### The axolotl
is a relative of the newt. It usually remains as a tadpole, even when it is breeding. In the wild it is only found in a few lakes in Mexico, which are polluted and being drained. It is domesticated as a pet.

### The Galapagos giant turtle
is confined to the Galapagos Islands in the Pacific. They were killed for their meat by sailors but now their main threats include competition from goats and attacks on their eggs by rats.

### The gharial
is a fish-eating crocodile from India, which came close to extinction. It was saved by removing and artificially incubating its eggs. The young gharials were then released into protected areas.

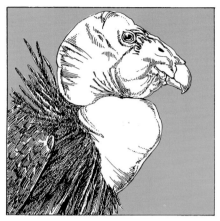

**The California condor**
is one of the rarest birds in the world. Some of the last remaining birds are being bred in captivity, and the first two condors to fly free in the wild were released in January 1992.

**The ivory-billed woodpecker**
was once hunted by North American Indians who made necklaces from its bill. Its habitat on the mainland was destroyed by European settlers and it only survives in Cuba.

**The St Helena earwig**
is confined to the remote island of St Helena in the Atlantic Ocean, where Napoleon was imprisoned. In 1988 an expedition failed to find any so it may well have become extinct.

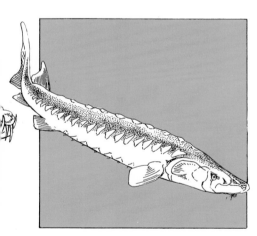

**The short-nosed sturgeon**
is found along the North American coast from New Brunswick, Canada to Florida and in large river channels. It is threatened by pollution and many have been found to have fin rot.

**The Philip Island hibiscus**
is one of the world's rarest plants and is found in two patches on an uninhabited Pacific island. Its seedlings were prevented from growing by rabbits and overcrowding from African olives.

**Leek orchids**
are known to number 80 species, which are found in Australia, New Zealand and New Caledonia. Four species are known to be extinct in Australia, where another 12 are rare or threatened.

# Index

**Photographic Credits:**
Cover and pages 6, 12 (both), 13, 15 (both), 16, 17, 20 (left), 21, 22, 23 (middle), 24, 26 and 28: Bruce Coleman; pages 4-5, 8 (both), 9, 11 (bottom), 20 (right), 25 (both) and 28-29: Planet Earth; page 7: Zoology Dept of the Natural History Museum; page 10-11: Peter Newark's Western Americana; pages 11 (top), 14, 18 and 19 (both): Survival Anglia; page 23 (top): Associated Press; page 27: Roger Wilson; page 29: Royal Botanical Gardens, Kew.

PRINTED IN BELGIUM BY
proost
INTERNATIONAL BOOK PRODUCTION